I0460849

FINDING MY VOICE

A SPIRITUAL JOURNEY

By Deb Crutcher

FINDING MY VOICE

A SPIRITUAL JOURNEY

DEB CRUTCHER

HOWLING WOLF PRESS

Copyright © 2025 by Deb Crutcher

Cover art by Lisa Rene Engelbart

All rights reserved.

No portion of this book may be reproduced in any form without written permission from the publisher or author, except as permitted by U.S. copyright law.

ISBN: 978-1-961703-07-0

ACKNOWLEDGEMENTS

My sincere gratitude to my beta readers, Steve Abney, MK Browning, Nancy Desmond, and Teresa Turner. A big thanks to the members of the Winter Haven Writers group, who gave me constructive critiques and kept me moving forward with my writing.

I want to give a big thanks to my editor and dear friend, Ellen Holder.

Finally, I want to thank my dear gifted friend, Miss Sharon Quinn, who provided guidance and support on my spiritual journey and encouraged me to tell my story through this book.

DEDICATION

For my spiritual leader, Sharon Quinn,
and for my helping guides and angels
who steered my hands while writing this book.

CONTENTS

INTRODUCTION

"scream
so that one day
a hundred years from now
another sister will not have to
dry her tears wondering
where in history
she lost her voice" —Jasmin Kaur

It began with a childhood innocence that disappeared too soon. Fear, uncertainty, unknowing, lack of guidance, and lack of confidence seeped into my life too early. Attending six different grade schools from the first to the fifth grade and living in seven different houses until I went to college was unsettling and confusing in my early years. I never understood why we moved so much when I was younger. Some of my relatives said it was because my mother was never happy where she was. One year she wanted to be near her family, the next she wanted nothing to do with them. When I was in the fifth grade, we finally settled in a small county of Western Kentucky in a resort area on the large man-made Kentucky Lake.

My life continued with many trials and errors with poor results. Unaware of my true self, I ran through life rushing ahead, jumping off cliffs without looking. Too many wrong choices, regrets, and dark shadows weighed me down.

This is my story, how I coped, what I did to overcome my life's hurdles, and how I found the courage, guidance, and determination to capture my fleeting true voice and never let it go again.

ONE

BEING GRATEFUL

Appreciate the freshness of every moment.

What are you grateful for? Many things come to mind when I'm asked this—my home and its beautiful lake view; nature with its whispering trees, tropical rainforests, colorful flowers, bodies of water; the galaxy full of twinkling stars; my dear friends and family; and Mother Earth.

But what are you really grateful for about yourself? Not your big blue beautiful eyes, shiny hair, shapely legs, or dancing skills. Dig deep into your personality, into your core. What are you most thankful for? Is it your honesty, integrity, loyalty, morality, or the ability to care for others? This is a thought-provoking question for all to ponder.

What I am most grateful for is my voice, my authentic true voice. I'm not talking about my ability to speak. I never had that problem. Most of my report cards had the note, "Excellent student. Talks too much."

In the third grade, our teacher warned a group of us to stop talking. When she threatened to tape our mouths shut, we just giggled. Soon, six of us found ourselves with a giant X of gray duct tape across our mouths.

We sat like that for about an hour, then went to lunch. The older students pointed and laughed at us as we walked the hall of shame. The tape was removed only after we received our lunch trays and sat down. Can you imagine if that situation occurred to third graders in a public school these days?

Knowing your true voice means you have the confidence to speak up for your beliefs, desires, and dislikes, knowing that your words are worthy. You speak with sincerity and honesty. A person with an authentic voice is accountable for their words and actions. Perhaps choosing speech-language pathology as my career was part of my destiny.

Throughout my life and my marriages, I almost owned my voice several times, then it slipped away again and again. It was a roller coaster of emotions, climbing and then sliding back down again. In one marriage I was completely silenced at times. One of my ex-husbands, in social situations, told me when to talk and what to say.

Most of the time, he said, "Just sit there and keep your mouth shut." All the while I watched him pretending to be someone he wasn't or trying to impress an investor when I knew he had no intentions of joining their project. He loved appearing important.

I finally found my voice and it's much stronger than before. It took years, but I will never lose it again. This is what happened to me, how I overcame the hurdles along my spiritual journey. Through four husbands and four divorces, here I am. One of the happiest and most content people you will ever meet.

TWO

PEELING THE ONION

Life is a balance between holding on and letting go.

T o begin my journey, I first had to learn to love myself. That sounds easy, but it's one of the hardest things I ever accomplished. Trolling through the dark sludge of the past—years of regrets, anger, and heartbreaks––was painful. It all needed to be purged to make room for love, joy, and happiness.

Stepping out of the darkness and into the light is a slow process like peeling layers of an onion. Many times, I wanted to quit or give up, but my stubbornness, curiosity, and determination pushed me forward. My mother used to say, "If you want Debbie to do something, just tell her she can't."

We must heal our emotional field to access a higher one. Otherwise, we are out of alignment. My mind was controlling my body. My body was hurting, and my soul was hiding behind all the debris I collected along the way. My mind, body, and soul had to be aligned to heal.

When we expand by cleaning out the past, we will have a larger container to receive positivity. We will always have a dark side, just as there will always be a light side. We can hold both negative and positive energies. The goal is to be aware and able to humanely neutralize the negative so that it does no harm.

When you are living a spiritual life, with self-love and kindness for yourself, negativity is easier to manage. Most of the time, the toxic behavior bounces off. Other times, I deal with the darkness, examine it, and ask, *Why does it affect me this way? What lesson is this teaching me?* Then I let it flow through me. No more denial or locking up those feelings.

THREE

POWER OF MEDITATION

*If you meditate alone, it's wonderful. If you meditate
with a group, it's as powerful as meditating seven days
in a row.*

Seventy-three percent of the planet is energy. Scientists have discovered that what they thought was empty space is an invisible nervous system, a woven network connecting everything. We are all connected through a big picture and part of the same whole. It makes sense that when we shift our energy we are moving and impacting the energy of the outside world.

Many lightworkers, people with high vibrational energy, believe that if enough of us shift to higher energy, we can have a positive effect on the entire planet and the chaotic environment we are currently experiencing. They have made a conscious decision to make the world a brighter place. They know that their presence has the potential to create positive changes.

Sandra Ingerman's book, *Walking in Light, The Everyday Empowerment of a Shamanic Life,* states, "In our culture, we tend to focus on methods and forget that the greatest way we can offer healing to the world is to become a vessel of love." Ms. Ingerman states that if enough people raise their vibrational energy level, we can positively affect Mother Earth.

While visiting Fairfield, Iowa, I heard a story about Maharishi Mahesh. When he was constructing his compound in Fairfield, an unexpected cold wave swept through the area. Temperatures were too cold for the planned concrete pour. He instructed thousands of his advanced followers to meditate together to raise the temperature. It was a success. It grew warm enough for the concrete to be poured and groomed.

Visiting the town of Fairfield was like watching an episode of *Twilight Zone.* People walked around in their flannel shirts and carried their water in glass jars. All were smiling and friendly, yet aloof as if they were in a trance.

Most of the residents of this town, including the mayor and his family, meditated using the Transcendental Meditation (TM) method. Because of this town's uniqueness, certain celebrities have visited, such as Oprah, Paul McCartney, and Matthew McConaughey.

In addition to the Maharishi International University, established in 1971 for consciousness-based education, the Yogi constructed twin golden meditation domes, each twenty thousand to twenty-five thousand square feet. Each dome holds one thousand people. There's one for men and another for women. The Maharishi brought thousands of young men from India and housed them in rows of barracks. Their only job was to meditate.

Group meditations in the domes occurred early in the morning and again in the evening before dinner. They say it was quite unusual and at times comical to see crowds of people rushing to the domes to arrive before the doors were closed and entrance was forbidden.

The Maharishi then built a Vedic City outside of town, where all homes were built according to specific Vedic architecture. This is where the rows of white barracks were located that housed the hundreds of young male meditators from India.

This unusual small town of just under ten thousand residents promoted spirituality and meditation, with a strange feeling of peacefulness.

FOUR

THE SEARCH FOR UNCONDITIONAL LOVE

"What you seek is seeking you." . . . Rumi

Throughout my marriage, I searched for unconditional love—love that I never received from my mother. Instead of allowing love to find me, I chased love, fearing that I would lose my partner's love if I did the wrong thing. Conversely, if I did something pleasing, I thought they would love me more.

Walking on eggshells, I tried to please everyone but myself. I gave to others, ignoring my needs and, at the same time, pushed resentment and pain down. Those demons never go away. They fester and eat you alive, causing anxiety, anger, confusion, and eventually health issues as it did with me.

I was treated by a psychologist after one of my divorces, and she suggested that I was marrying men with similar characteristics to my mother because I was comfortable with that type of verbal abuse and neglect. I kept repeating my past, my mistakes, and choosing the wrong mate.

Viewing my childhood photos, I found none with my mother's arms around me. I don't recall the words "I love you" coming from her mouth. I do remember words spewed such as: "How could you be so stupid? You are so clumsy. How in the world could you do something so dumb?"

Instead of encouragement, when I announced I was changing my major to speech-language pathology, she replied, "Why on Earth do you want to work so hard?"

I will never forget the time I flew in from New York, after not seeing my parents for a year. The first words that flew from her mouth were, "Debbie, where is ya' lipstick?" Then, "How long are you staying; hope no longer than three days."

I was the third of four children, one sister ten years older and a brother eight years older. When I was three, my older sister needed emergency brain surgery. My mother stayed with her in a special children's hospital several hours away. I spent the next few glorious weeks with my aunt and uncle on their farm. They had no children and spoiled me like their own.

When my mother came to retrieve me weeks later, my aunt said I screamed and cried when she put me in the car. I think even at that early age, I knew where I was safest. I paid for that rejection of her until the day she passed away.

I spent many childhood summers and school breaks on that farm. Some of my fondest memories are spending time with my aunt and uncle, running free down the country dirt lane with scents of honeysuckle permeating the air.

Soon after, my older sister and I were back home Mother delivered my younger sister. From that point, our complicated relationship grew worse as my mother aged.

One of my biggest disappointments as a child was when I was a Brownie in the third grade. Our troop leader announced, "You are ready to gain your wings to the Girl Scouts. We are planning the pinning ceremony next month. Everybody, please have your uniforms ready."

I had only been a Brownie for a couple of months. Luckily for me, the meetings after school were close enough for me to walk home. My father worked nights and slept during the day or worked on his father's farm; transportation was left to my mother. She would never allow me to participate in after-school activities that required her to pick me up. This policy continued until the day I could drive myself to school. This was confusing since my mother had been active in my older sibling's school activities, volunteering as homeroom mother and even president of the PTA.

The hope of joining the Girl Scouts was exciting. I looked forward to the cookie drives, earning badges, and belonging to a special group. My dreams were crushed when my mother said no. There was no money for a uniform. There would be no green skirt and matching shirt, no green socks, no beret. My heart was broken. I was not going to be a Girl Scout.

There were no crying fits or temper tantrums, no questions, or "Why not?" When my parents said no, especially due to finances, that was the final answer.

Was I a Brownie? I never wore the uniform. I was biding my time until Girl Scouts. What I don't understand is why my parents let me continue with Brownies, so hopeful, when they knew I was never going to be a Girl Scout.

FIVE

LIVING A SPIRITUAL LIFE

Life is not a matter of milestones but of moments.

W hat does it mean to be a spiritual person? Uninformed and judgmental people might say it's practicing "witchy" craft or working with the dark side, doing Satan's work. One evening as women arrived for a sisterhood gathering at my home, a nosy neighbor asked if I was having "one of those seances." She declined when I invited her to join us.

Being spiritual is living a kind, compassionate life full of love for all of humanity, nature, animals, and most importantly for yourself. Spirituality is about being awake, aware, and conscious of your environment and your emotions. Without love, kindness, and caring for ourselves, one cannot be truly happy with someone else.

Spiritual people don't seek another to fulfill their needs. They seek others to share the experience of happiness they already have. This releases friends, family, or partners from the impossible burden of providing happiness. Awakening is knowing what's always been there, your special light. Let your ego retire and let your true nature shine. Seek happiness within, not outward.

When I am asked on a questionnaire or in person about my religious choice, I reply that I am spiritual. I do not believe in organized religions. I was raised in a Baptist environment, baptized at the age of twelve, and forced to go to church every Sunday morning, most Sunday evenings, and every local summer vacation Bible school, no matter what the denomination. Begging my mother to let me stay home on Sunday nights, so I could watch *The Wonderful World of Disney*, was rarely successful.

How could I forget those week-long revivals, lasting late into the night with some visiting fire-and-brimstone preacher droning on, warning about the angry side of God? Finally, some so-called sinner walked forward to repent his sins and be saved, so we could go home. I used to wonder how one could be excused from their evil ways so easily.

The Baptist Church I attended was strict. No musical instruments, except the piano or organ, were allowed. Women could not wear pants to church or vote on any of the issues. When our teen group wanted to plan a picnic by the lake, we were told we could have the picnic, but there could be no swimming. The Bible stated that mixed bathing was forbidden.

I recognized hypocrisy and contradictions in the church around the time I entered high school. However, until I left for college I continued to attend Sunday school and church services to appease my mother. In one of those Sunday school classes when I was in my teens, the teacher made a profound statement. She said, "If you were on an island and the only book you had to read was the Bible and you read that Bible and followed all of the teachings, you would be a Baptist." I didn't question my teacher at the time, but that statement piqued my curiosity and my skepticism.

To illustrate how stern this church was, there's the joke, "Do you know why Baptists don't make love standing up? Because they don't want anyone to think they are dancing."

At that time, the West Kentucky county where I grew up and most of the surrounding areas were dry, meaning no alcohol was sold. Public dancing was also illegal. My senior high school class was forced to have their prom in a neighboring county, one hour away, so we could legally dance.

In my mid-thirties, after a divorce, I was in search of guidance and set out to explore different religions. Thinking that the church and its activities were a great place to meet people, I attended services at a Lutheran, Episcopal, and Unity Church, and a couple of Buddhist services. Unfortunately, none of these religions touched my soul. I did not want to be connected to a belief that God was vengeful. I was looking for a loving spirit, a forgiving deity.

For the next several years, I stopped searching; I was in a rocky marriage. When people asked me about my religion, I replied, "I'm spiritual." For me, that meant I wasn't connected to any religion. One thing is for sure, I wasn't practicing spirituality either.

To be honest, I was judgmental and a bit resentful of people who claimed to be religious. Now, I accept that a spiritual person can also be religious and that a religious person can also be spiritual. Two examples are Mahatma Gandhi and Mother Teresa. They were both driven by spiritual visions and the belief in oneness, truth, and unconditional love for all.

SIX

SPIRITUALITY ALL AROUND WHILE I SLEPT

"Mad with thirst, you can't drink from the stream run-ning close by your face. You are like a pearl on the deep bottom wondering inside the shell, Where's the ocean?"

Rumi

When I was younger, hints of spirituality were all around me, but I was still asleep. When living in France, I accompanied my friend, who had unresolved health issues, to a ladies' home for possible treatment. When we arrived midmorning, I noticed a small altar on the floor in the living room. It had a Buddha statue, with a flower, a small bowl of nuts, and burning incense. At that time, I thought incense was just for fragrance and wondered why she would be burning it in the morning by this statue. My friend and I were a bit confused and alarmed, due to our unawareness of this practice.

Later, I discovered this lady was a spiritual healer. In Buddhism and Hinduism, gifts of food and beauty are offered to honor and please the gods. I'm sure many of you have seen this type of altar in some nail salons.

SEVEN

BALI

Open your heart to receive unlimited love.

On my trip to Bali in October 2016, I noticed every home and business had a shrine of beautiful flowers decorating all their deities. Statues of Shiva, Buddha, and Ganesha (the Hindu deity who is the remover of obstacles) were draped with marigold necklaces everywhere you looked. Many homes had a private garden of flowers for their daily decorations and many ceremonies.

The Balinese people were gentle, honest, loving, and industrious. They were always busy: Sweeping, cleaning, gathering flowers, and immersed in their traditions. They didn't have much, but they didn't seem to want much—an excellent attribute for all of humanity.

One of the most powerful experiences in Bali was the Sacred Black Moon Water-Cleansing ceremony. This was the time of the new moon celebrated at the ancient Tira Ampule Temple.

This sacred ceremony, performed to clear one's karma, is not easy to describe. It's one of those things you have to experience to truly understand. It's a physical movement, but the internal shift is the important one.

As soon as we arrived, women surrounded us, selling blessings for the high priest. We brought our own basket of offerings prepared by the kitchen where we stayed. We were guided to locker rooms, where we exchanged our clothes for a thin rented sarong, taking off all undergarments. The sarong was tied around our neck. The men were bare-chested with a sarong covering their legs. We all wore the required colorful sashes around our waists to remind us to curtail our egos. Our hair had to be tied up. This was a serious sacred ceremony. Every ritual had to be followed, or you would not be allowed to participate.

We lined up at the steps of this long, narrow concrete pool filled with water. People moved from a series of fifteen sprockets with flowing, crystal-clear water. Our Shaman leader instructed us as follows: With hands in prayer position state our intention, wash our heads three times, and then dunk our heads completely under the water, move to the next sprocket, and repeat until we reach the end.

One by one, we moved down the mossy steps—the chill of the water took my breath away. My sarong floated to the top as I stood in water up to my chest. The coldness of the water contrasted with the brilliant heat of the sun. A nice balance.

At first, I barely put my head under the water. Then my prayers grew longer and more intense. I lowered my head, letting the cold water completely cover me and run down my back and bare shoulders. By the time I was at spigot number ten, I was in tears. I was releasing anger and clearing obstacles. Years of rage and disappointments surrounding my mother surfaced, and I was letting go.

Most of the people in our group were crying or laughing with joy. What a wonderful, memorable experience. Water is one of the best ways to clear your energy centers. When water flows over your head, it clears blockages from your crown chakra. These obstacles could result in brain fog or mental stagnation.

EIGHT

MONKS IN MARATHON

Smile to a new day.

While living in Marathon in the Florida Keys, I walked into the town's only combination health food and bookstore. I was surprised when a group of orange-robed men with shaved heads entered the store with handmade trinkets and cards for sale. *Monks in the Keys?*

Before long the crowd settled on the floor and huddled into the small space as these men played beautiful crystal bowls and began to chant. Not knowing how to react, I observed others sitting cross-legged with their eyes closed, so I did the same. Listening to their deep overtone chanting with those powerful harmonizing sounds of the bowls was magical. Years later, I realized that was my first sound bath.

These Tibetan Monks traveled every year to the Keys, stopping along the way. They spent days in Key West creating a massive, colorful, intricate mandala with sand. A mandala is a geometric design, always in a circle, which represents the universe and the point where we are all connected.

Another example of how spirituality was practically jumping in my face, was when I enrolled in the twelve-week workshop, "The Artist's Way, A Spiritual Path to Higher Creativity." The program, developed by Julia Cameron, was led by a local published author, Rosalind Brackenbury in Key West.

It was one of the best self-help programs I have ever experienced. In the weekly group of twenty participants, there were many gifted spiritual people. The goal of the workshop was to help people free their creativity by using a spiritual pathway. It focused on self-love, exploring your dreams, desires, fears, limiting beliefs, and guilt. The program is based on the fact that creativity lives in all of us.

One of my favorite exercises was taking myself on a weekly artist's date. The date could be something as simple as buying some crayons and a sketch pad; visiting a museum; or incorporating silly, fun things into your day. Some of the dates I chose were to snuggle in bed with my cat and a good book, spend time in the historical section of the Key West Library, stroll through the Botanical Gardens in Key West, and walk on the most serene beach of Bahia Honda State Park.

This class inspired me to publish my first book of poetry, *Living on the Edge*, and to move forward with my dream of moving to France. Being around higher-energy people in this group renewed my curiosity and excitement about spirituality.

NINE

IN FRANCE

May you always find the light within and have the courage to take a chance.

While we struggled through our divorce, my third ex had a bad habit of showing up unannounced at odd times. I was living in Marathon; he lived in Boca Raton. For example, one time I got out of the shower, and he was standing in my bathroom. Another time I was attending a one-day workshop in Key Largo, and he showed up midday. I surmised that he was checking up on me, trying to catch me in a lie. My husband had trust issues with everyone. I suppose when you are not trustworthy and you're a liar, then you expect others to be the same.

The urge was growing to get far away from him and anything that reminded me of the unpleasant memories associated with that marriage. Especially the last situation, where my husband announced that he had gotten a young lady pregnant with twins. The young lady was a streetwalker who roamed the streets of Fort Lauderdale, and he had gotten quite attached to her. For a while, he thought he would be starting a new life, until he found out she had returned to the streets and her drug habits.

Three lawyers and four years later, after my divorce from this twenty-one-year marriage, I moved to France. I needed a new environment, a new beginning. After placing a few precious items in storage and receiving my visa, I was off to my rented apartment in Aix-en-Provence, France.

Aix is known as the Paris of Provence due to its chic stores, rich art, cultural heritage, beautiful architecture, and many historical fountains. There were markets somewhere in the village almost every day. My heart and mind were always open to new surprises waiting for me around the corner as I walked along the cobblestone streets.

Soon after arriving, one Sunday morning I was strolling the wide avenue, Cours Mirabeau, which was shaded by a canopy of tall plane trees with maple-shaped leaves. Sundays in France were special. Most establishments were closed except for a few restaurants that catered to large families and their long lunches. It was beautiful to see families enjoying an unhurried meal with well-behaved children and, at times, a disciplined dog lying under the table.

Of course, the boulangeries were emitting that delicious smell of freshly cooked bread for Sunday dinners before they closed for the day. I saw fathers with strollers, enjoying their quiet day off. Sundays in France were indeed a day of rest. I learned quickly to pick up something for dinner, knowing that most restaurants or markets would be closed on Sunday evenings.

As I walked away from the main street, I saw a group gathering in a nearby park. They were preparing for an exercise of some type. I approached the young man who was organizing the event and asked if he spoke English and if I could join them. His English was mingled with French, but he invited me to join. He placed me up front and said to watch and follow his movements. That was my first Qigong class.

The ancient study of Qigong uses breath control, coordinated with slow, peaceful movements. This technique is helpful with meditating. After that day, I attended Qigong classes with this leader in his studio three mornings a week. I'll admit it was challenging, not knowing the language, but the teacher was good at translating now and then. Arriving early, I took a spot up front and followed along the best I could. This internal martial art was my new love.

While in France, my thirst for spirituality grew as I continued reading and researching. I was going deeper and longer with my meditations and beginning to see visions. At times, I lay on the floor for what seemed like hours, trying to reach that sweet spot of nothingness that some call the gap, the spot of authentic pure truth. Sometimes I reached it, other times not. It was frustrating and rewarding at the same time.

TEN

RETURN TO FLORIDA

Flow with ease, like water; bloom without struggle, like a rose.

After a fun, inspiring, and educational year in France, I moved back to Delray Beach, Florida. After spending most of my life around water, being landlocked in France was not for me. The surf, sand, and warm sunshine of Florida were calling me home. I also healed to the point that I wasn't going to allow anyone to drive me away from my home, my friends, and the place where I had lived and worked for over forty years.

Back in Florida, I continued my Qigong practice with a wonderful teacher, Dr. Nick Kusturic, who was also an acupuncturist. Continuing this practice three times a week, I was so intrigued by this modality that I set a goal of receiving a teaching certificate. I traveled to Boston for a workshop with the grandmaster, Mantak Chia, then a week of Qigong instruction at a retreat in the Berkshire mountains, and finally traveled to Asheville, North Carolina to attend sessions with Michael Winn, who was part of the Healing Tao.

Although I had completed only sixty percent of training toward my certificate, I was permitted by my teacher to teach the basics. I put an ad in the paper and the local magazines and posted flyers around town. It stated that, on Saturday morning, Qigong classes would be held outside under a huge shade tree on the grounds of the historical old square in Delray Beach.

For several months, three to six people showed up and practiced outside with me. One day a lady called from a Fifty-Five-Plus Community and wanted to hire me for once-a-week Qigong lessons. It was rewarding to share my gift with this group of ladies. We met for three months until the snowbirds flew North.

It took me years of "ah-ha" moments to learn more about myself and what I needed. I related the process to the peeling back of an onion. Little by little, layers fell away. It got messy. I cried and wanted to give up because it was too painful. There were so many confusing things I did not understand. But I had to get to that core.

ELEVEN

DRUM CIRCLE AT CRYSTAL GARDEN

Unfurl your sail and drift . . . Let go.

The first full-moon drum circle I attended at the Crystal Garden in Boynton Beach, Florida, with two of my best friends, was the real awakening of my spiritual journey. We called ourselves the Moon Shadow Gals because, for several years, we met for the full moon rising over the Atlantic Ocean each month. One night, while enjoying the bright moon shining across the waves, we each came up with a challenge.

Each of us thought of an activity that would take the others out of their comfort zone. One friend chose for us to get tattoos, which we all did at the same time one Valentine's Day. Another took us to a special movie, showing the life and music of Neil Young. The movie lasted till midnight, which was way past our bedtime.

It was my idea to go to a drum circle. I was fifty-nine at the time. As we entered the room with twenty or so people sitting in a circle surrounding a huge powwow drum, I was intimidated. My friends and I were new to this activity and did not know what to expect. The leader called in the spirits of the archangels and explained that we were only to walk clockwise around the sacred circle. We each were given a small drum or tambourine to join in the gathering. She said that if the feeling was right, come to the center of the circle and pound away. Before we started drumming, we took a moment to silently set our intentions.

I watched people walk to that big drum and hit it with all their energy—hair and sweat slinging as if they were in a trance. I took two turns beating on that drum until tears flowed. Something inside me shifted, awakened. I felt joy and a new sense of freedom.

TWELVE

SEARCHING CONTINUES

Eyes open would not be forced closed again.

A fter the drum experience, I feverishly set out on a search for all things spiritual. One winter when my brother was visiting me, I searched for an activity we could enjoy. He was interested in Native American Indian culture, so when I saw a drum circle scheduled on the Meet-Up app, I inquired with the host. She gave me directions and said we were welcome. Grandfather Rick, from the Cherokee nation, would be leading the circle. Women were to cover their arms and legs.

My brother and I drove west toward the Everglades. We were in some deep, remote, swampy area with dirt roads. We saw a nice, well-lit ranch house as I maneuvered my Prius into the yard. Our car was the only one there. My brother turned to me and said, "We don't know what we're walking into. We could be murdered."

I replied, "Our religious mother is turning over in her grave knowing we're doing this."

We sat there a few moments, and some other guests arrived, so we joined in. It was awkward and uncomfortable, not knowing any of the other guests or what to expect. We all took off our shoes and entered a room with chairs set in a circle.

Grandfather Rick, as it turned out, was from Arkansas and looked like a redneck, not an Indian chief. We were handed a small flat drum. He explained that the drumbeat he initiated must be followed exactly. After we honored the animals that sacrificed their skins for the instrument, Grandfather Rick began to beat his drum, and we all followed along.

Well, almost all of us followed. The young lady sitting next to me was also new to the group. She got into the drumming and started her own beat, swinging her head and body with the rhythm and smiling. Suddenly, Grandfather Rick stopped drumming and, with a stern voice, explained that she must follow the exact beat. Poor girl just kept hitting her drum to a beat of her own. It was difficult to suppress my giggles. I doubt if Grandfather Rick asked her back.

My brother and I wouldn't return to this cult-like group either. As soon as the drumming was over, we gave our love donation and hit the road, laughing at the entire situation. This was not the spiritual group I was looking for.

THIRTEEN

RED TENT

Commit to loving yourself.

I attended any meditation groups I could find. I took a one-day meditation class on primordial meditation and joined a sisterhood group at the Red Tent. The Red Tent was a healing arts center for women. Their services included new moon circles, massages for pregnant women, yoga, Reiki therapy, and various other holistic healings.

As mentioned in the Bible, the Red Tent was a place where women went during their time of the monthly periods and to give birth. The older women joined the group, sharing stories of their ancestors, singing songs, and being joyful. Since no men were allowed, it gave the women a much-needed break from their arduous duties of caring for their families.

Our monthly Red Tent gatherings were led by a Yogi master who was an astrologer. These gatherings took place around the time of the new moon, also called the dark moon. Women have been gathering in the darkness, at the time of the new moon, for centuries.

The mystery of the darkness compares to the mystery of women. Our sexual organs are in the dark, out of site. We grow humans in the dark womb. There has always been this mystery of the woman which the other gender doesn't always understand.

In the past women have gathered in church groups, quilting bees, or cookie-baking parties. Women need women, for we are the healers, the ones who nurture. We listen without the need to fix each other.

Our meetings were uplifting with positive themes of love. We meditated, danced, and shared our intentions for the upcoming month. New moons are for setting intentions, whereas full moons are for celebrating the progress of those goals and to release them to the universe.

FOURTEEN

SISTERHOOD GROUPS

The more we give, the more we receive.

I wasn't sure what it meant to be a spiritual person; however, I believed I was on the right path. The group at the Red Tent grew to over thirty women, most of whom were much younger. I decided, with the blessing of the leader, to start a small group of friends who were closer to my age. Our desires, needs, and experiences were different than the younger ladies who were starting their careers or families. The responsibility of being the group leader gave me a great opportunity to explore and discover various ways to express and share our spirituality.

The yearning to share my knowledge and to inspire others to explore self-love was intense. We shared stories, fears, accomplishments, and desires. We celebrated Mother Earth by offering her gifts, honored International Women's Day, and meditated, danced, laughed, and cried. Our monthly New Moon sisterhood meetings continued for three years until I relocated to Central Florida.

FIFTEEN

TIME WITH DEEPAK CHOPRA

Love yourself as the most precious thing in the universe,
because you are.

In my research on meditation and spirituality, I found a twenty-one-day meditation challenge with Oprah and Deepak Chopra. The goal was to meditate every day on these guided meditations. Never missing a day, his program helped me establish a daily, disciplined routine of meditation. If you can get used to Deepak's accent, his voice is very soothing and perfect for guiding you into the bliss.

After reading two of Chopra's books, *The Seven Spiritual Laws of Success* and *The Book of Secrets: Hidden Dimensions of Your Life*, I was determined to learn more from this spiritual leader. In April, 2014, I traveled to Carlsbad, California, and attended the week-long Seduction of Spirit workshop at the Deepak Chopra Center. Meditating with a group of three hundred-plus people three to five times a day took some getting used to. By the end of the week, I was reaching that sweet spot every time.

Every day we had different spiritual speakers, such as Caroline Myss, Marianne Williamson, Byron Katie, and Davidji. Deepak was very excited to share his positive recent research on how meditation affects the brain.

Earlier in the week, I met a lady from Jupiter, Florida, just thirty minutes from where I lived in South Florida. One night I was late for dinner and having difficulty finding an empty seat when I spotted the lady from Jupiter. I sat down with eight other women and started chatting away. I noticed everyone was attentive to me, but no one responded. They just nodded their heads. Then someone pointed to a button they were all wearing, which read: We are in Silence, Please Respect.

I remembered there was a group of about fifty participants who choose to enroll in the Silent Program for three days. They were not allowed to communicate verbally, and only in writing if necessary. It is a practice to go inside oneself, quieten the mind, and remove all devices and distractions until the outside noise fades away, leaving your true self.

I apologized and offered to go sit somewhere else, not wanting to interfere with their program. Using gestures, they indicated that they wanted me to stay and continue. I told stories of my online dating experiences. Instead of finding a prince to kiss, they were all toads on a log. I had a captive audience and kept them laughing throughout their entire meal.

Chopra's method of meditating used a mantra that you continuously repeated as you meditated. When I first arrived at the reception, I was asked the exact time and place where I was born. A computer program calculated and determined the sound I would have heard the exact moment I was born in that particular city at that specific time. This was my personal mantra, which you are not to share with anyone. I didn't understand why I had to keep it a secret, but I did. Maybe they didn't want us to know that we all had the same mantra. That was my cynicism kicking in. The week at the Chopra Centre taught me a great deal about spirituality.

One day when Deepak took the stage, in his deep, soothing voice he said, "It's all about love. Love is the answer."

Huh, easy for you to say. You are surrounded by your loving wife, your children, your associates; you have a lot of love around you. What about someone like me who doesn't have anyone to love them?

I didn't understand what he meant. I was a bit resentful that he would make this statement when it seemed to exclude many lonely people. It took many years before I realized he was talking about love for yourself, which eventually flows out to everything and everyone around you.

SIXTEEN

EXPLORING MEDITATIONS

"You had the power all along, my dear." Glinda

A few weeks after returning from the Chopra Center, I researched and experimented with several different types of meditation. I read more books, sought out any spiritual activity in the area, and continued my daily morning meditations along with my daily journaling. I noticed that meditating in the afternoon gave me as much energy as a cup of coffee. People commented on how relaxed and at peace I seemed. Everything around me was more vivid. I noticed details instead of just barreling through the day.

My Qigong master told us to be like cotton on the outside, feeling and absorbing energy, and metal on the inside, with a strong structure underneath. So many people put armor up around them for protection. I did. Shedding that armor was crucial for love to penetrate. A softer, more observant me emerged. This is what meditation did for me.

Since we have over sixty thousand thoughts a day, it is impossible to clear our minds. Memories, past conversations, fears, and plans are swirling around. When thoughts arise, instead of focusing on them, let them float away like clouds. The goal is to achieve stillness. When we surrender to the silence, or as it is often called, "the gap," that's where our true self lies.

When going within, set an intention, ask a question, and ask for guidance from the spirit. I say, "I am requesting, spirit." When I am thinking of a problem or a situation, I go into mediation with questions such as, "Why did I react that way? How could I have responded differently? Why am I having these negative feelings? What do I need to hear at this moment?"

Many times, the answers to my questions don't come immediately, but if I stay present and open to receive, a response will appear in the future. Give gratitude to the spirits for their guidance and wisdom on your journey, and all the shifts, adjustments, and new habits you have experienced.

When you go into your happy place as you meditate, whether you visualize yourself at the beach, in the mountains, forest, or floating on gentle, rocking waves (which is one of my favorites) take that peacefulness and that energy with you throughout the day.

There will be times when you are hurried, someone pulls out in front of you, someone at work is a jerk, your kids are misbehaving, and the phone won't stop ringing. That's when you take a deep breath, let it out, and take a moment to go back to that happy place and feel that peace again. Pause and say to yourself, "I am loved; I am enough. Everything is exactly as it should be." Let go of the tension, stress, and negativity.

Many meditations begin with breathing techniques. Deep diaphragmatic breathing is a proven method for decreasing stress. A deep breath through the nose, with a short pause then a slow exhale through the mouth is the most common method.

When learning scuba diving in 1979, I learned that smooth, rhythmic breathing was an important part of training for safety and conservation of air. It was a bit comical watching other divers struggle with their buoyance control, flailing their arms as if they were swimming. They eventually used up their air before the dive was over. For me, diving was one of the most relaxing things I did. My goal was to move with the flow of the ocean. I clasped my hands and held them to my chest while gently kicking my fins to maneuver through the reefs.

One of my partners was such a heavy breather that he would "buddy breathe" off my tank, using my octopus regulator, giving him a few extra minutes underwater. As we moved as one, it was a bit restrictive for me. Ironically, this was husband number three, who also restricted my speech and most of my behavior.

Learning to meditate is comparable to the breathing process you learn in scuba diving. The harder you tried to control your movements, the more difficult it became while preventing the outcome you wanted. When I wanted to rise above an obstacle such as a giant sea fan or a rising coral head, I took a deep breath and slowly floated up and over. Then to descend, I slowly exhaled.

This same slow, rhythmic breathing is used in meditating and Qigong. Now I strive to use this "going with the flow" technique in my daily life. If an obstacle appears, I rise above it, deep breathe, and go with the flow.

Some meditations use different rhythms of breathing, sometimes taking breaths in rapid succession, then slowing down and visualizing your breath as you inhale and exhale. The idea is to focus on anything but the brain chatter.

These same techniques are used in grounding and calming activities. Taking a deep diaphragmatic breath through the nose, holding it, then exhaling slowly through the mouth, making sure that the exhale is longer than the inhale is a proven method to aid in meditation as well as decreasing stress and anxiety. Residual or stale air builds up in our lungs, and deep breathing helps to make room for fresh oxygen.

Dr. Joe Dispenza teaches a breathing technique in his meditations that activates the pineal gland. Dispenza has several books, and he lectures worldwide on this healing technique. The first book I read (and thoroughly enjoyed) was, *Breaking the Habit of Being Yourself.*

Daily meditations are vital in living a spiritual life. Going within can also be achieved by being in nature, loving yourself, and finding ways to spread that love to the universe. The purpose of meditating is not to tune out and get away from it all, but to tune in, and get in touch. It's a technique to get in the space between your thoughts.

SEVENTEEN

BEING IN THE NOW

Take your hands off the wheel and coast for a while.

I kept hearing about being in the now. I was confused. *What does that mean? Where am I, if I am not in the now? I'm here, not there.* I bought the audiobook, *The Power of Now* by Echart Tolle. I found his book interesting and helpful. However, listening to his dry, monotone voice put me to sleep. Some things, at least for me, are easier to understand with experience and time. Grasping the concept of "now" was a skill that took me many years.

To be in the now, you must lift one leg, step from the past into the present, and hopefully soar into the future. For me, eliminating the memories spinning around in my head was tough and painful. It is impossible to be in the now while living in the past, letting memories haunt and interfere with your current life. Likewise, if you spend too much time thinking or worrying about the future, you're not living in the present moment.

The past is gone; it's over. As footprints in the sand vanish in the surf, let your past float away. Forgiveness, compassion, gratitude, and love were my guides.

I learned that when someone triggered or irritated me, I paused. Instead of reacting, I responded with intention. I needed to be reminded that I could control my actions but not control the results of those actions. Allowing love and kindness to guide my words and actions was key. Coming back to things I could control and accept was important. When reconnecting to my internal energy, my own power, and the ability to move in the direction that best served me at the moment was an important lesson to learn—a new habit to establish. Forcing connections with people who don't see the value of having you is pointless. Today, when I recognize noxious people in my life, I quietly let them go, with love, and continue on my path.

There came a point in my journey where I felt like I couldn't go any further without guidance. I had so many questions. Finding a spiritual leader to guide me through this process was crucial. A trusted friend, a guru, a spiritual leader, or a religious person who shares your beliefs to help you on your path is invaluable.

Of course, no one can do the work for you, but they can provide techniques and confirm your progress. Each challenge I faced and overcame made space for increased energy. My goal was to transform myself into someone who rides the wave, rather than being the victim.

Looking back, so much of my life was pushing through challenges, unaware of the details of my surroundings. Today, I walk with my eyes, mind, and heart open.

EIGHTEEN

GROUNDING

"Forget not that the Earth delights to feel your bare feet, and the winds long to play with your hair."
Kahil Gibran

Another word often discussed in groups was "grounding." This word is common in martial arts, especially Qigong. In Qigong, your feet stay grounded like the roots of a tree. Grounding helps us shed any negative energy we have picked up. If we are in a chaotic, busy, perhaps toxic environment, we need a way to rid ourselves of this negativity.

Those with a greater awareness of the spiritual path might be affected more deeply than others. It is easier for people with elevated energy to notice when they are out of balance and need to realign. Grounding gives us a sense of calming, centering, and balancing.

It is best done in nature, where we can benefit from the oxygen freely given to us by the trees and plants. Because of their benefit of removing toxins and providing oxygen, my home is filled with plants, especially in my bedroom.

Slow down, be in nature, and consciously connect to the environment as you stroll. Know that you are walking over a network of roots that are connecting an underground communication system for trees. Research has shown great benefits for body and soul from being in nature. It decreases blood pressure, stress hormones, and depression.

Thich Nhat Hanh, a Vietnamese monk and peace activist said, "Walk as if your feet were kissing Mother Earth. Walk with gratitude, reverence, calm, and respect."

Most of the time we hike through the woods on autopilot without paying attention to our surroundings, or the details. Step into the woods or forest, among the trees with intentions, leaving technology behind. The path is in front of you. Trees have wisdom, if we only take the time to quiet our minds and to listen. Eddie Cantor expresses it this way: "Slow down and enjoy life. It's not only the scenery you miss by going too fast—you also miss the sense of where you are going and why."

In Japan, the ancient practice of shinrin-yoku, or forest bathing, has become very popular. It is a therapeutic healing practice of disconnecting from the outside world and sitting in a forest using all of your senses to connect with your surroundings. It is about engaging with nature through sight, hearing, taste, smell, and touch.

Today, I walk through the woods barefoot, with all senses open. I see and feel the movement all around and under me. I feel the cool breeze cleansing me. I hear the bamboo trees chatter as they rub together. Birds soar and land on nearby branches and we gaze at each other, their beautiful colors reflected by the sunlight. The calls of the owl, the whippoorwill, and the dove soothe me. The musty smell of decomposing leaves and organic matter drifts around me. The fresh air feels cool on my tongue.

With reverence, I gaze at the top of the massive trees. Trees that have been here long before me, with their intertwining branches reaching out to each other. I feel the texture of the tree's bark and leave my hand on its trunk to feel its energy. I stop, listen, see, feel, touch, smell and taste. This is being grounded and in the now.

We don't all have a forest to walk in or have the time to go to the woods. There are various other ways to ground oneself. Several crystals are used for grounding and clearing negative energy, such as sunstone, kyanite, obsidian, aquamarine, lapis lazuli, tourmaline, and selenite, to mention a few.

Crystals that hold Earth's energy need to be recharged by letting them soak in the full moon's glow. Be sure and remove them when the sun rises, so they don't fade. Depending on how often and where your crystals are used, they need cleansing. This is accomplished by smudging with smoke or cleansing with soap and water. Crystals that end with "ite," such as selenite, will dissolve in water, so use other methods to cleanse. Placing them in Mother Earth is another way to detoxify your crystals.

Many light workers who work with a variety of people use these crystals, between seeing their clients, to clear the energy field. Depending on what I am doing, I carry some type of crystal with me at all times, and I sleep with a few under my pillow which provides for a more restful night.

Another way to ground yourself is with conscious breathing. Visualize your breath as it fills your lungs, hold your breath for two seconds, then slowly exhale making your exhale longer than your inhale. Doing this breathing exercise several times can reduce stress while creating a calm feeling. At the same time, feel anchored. Feel the weight of your body against the ground or the chair you are sitting in. As your feet touch the ground, imagine they are rooted deep in Mother Earth.

Creative expression such as painting, writing, journaling, and music can all be grounding methods. Staring at a lighted candle's flame for a few minutes while getting in touch with your body is a grounding method. There are also electrical grounding mats available that many people use under their feet as they work. My spiritual leader takes a volcanic ash bath to neutralize any negative energy.

NINETEEN

SMUDGING

The greatest treasure you will ever find is the light within you.

Smudging, also called saging, is an ancient ritual used among many cultures, including the Native Americans, healers, spiritual gatherings, and religious groups. The ritual of smudging can be defined as "spiritual house cleaning." In theory, the smoke attaches itself to negative energy and toxins. The smoke clears the area by releasing it into another space where it will be regenerated into positive energy. If possible, open a window to allow the negative energy to escape.

When preparing for a ceremony, smudging is used to calm the mind, remove negative thoughts, and aid in being present. When we smudge our sacred space, we open our souls and call upon the compassionate spirits of the land, our spirit guides, and angels to join us in our circle. Clearing negative energy and thoughts helps us to feel more centered and protected from the world.

To smudge, you need the material you are going to burn, a lighter or match, a feather, and a container to catch the ashes. Sage is the most popular cleansing herb, but palo santo, lavender, lemongrass, cedar, or other herbs may be used.

To honor all of Earth's elements in the ceremony, a seashell such as an abalone may be used which represents water. The herbs are from Mother Earth, the smoke and feather represent air, and the fire is used to ignite the material.

Like burning incense, light the bundle of herbs at an angle and let them burn for a few seconds, then blow out the flame, so a smoldering of smoke is emitted. Fan the smoke with your feather as you move around the area to be cleansed.

Give purpose to your ritual, by stating a prayer or mantra. I say something like, "Please cleanse this space of negative energy. Only positivity is welcomed here. Bring love, joy, happiness, and protection."

Smudging is used to prepare for ceremonies or meditation, to remove pollutants from your home, and to cleanse yourself and your objects. Workers who deal with lots of people, especially those who shake hands or travel, benefit from regular smudging.

A 2006 study published in the "Journal of Ethnopharmacology" found that the air-cleansing effect from smudging can last up to thirty days. My home was regularly smudged during the pandemic scare.

When I have been around a large group of people, such as a concert, play, or shopping, I sage myself when I get home. When people have been in my house, or there is someone around who is sick or depressed, cleansing takes place. It is also a great uplifting technique when you are feeling low.

TWENTY

FALSE PROPHETS

A rolling stone gathers no moss.

Beware of false prophets. I wish I had known this. What is a false prophet? He or she is a person who lies, who is deceptive, fraudulent, and misleading. They claim to have a divine connection, and some speak as if they were a teacher of spirituality. I've met a few of these along my journey––one in particular. I was so anxious to meet a like-minded partner that I was blinded by the red-flag warnings.

When I first saw his picture on Facebook, he was wearing a Nehru jacket and was in a meditation pose—sitting with legs crossed, palms upward. "A man who meditates," I said to myself. After sharing on Facebook and phone calls, I made plans to visit him.

He said he was in a temporarily difficult financial position because he was at the end of a divorce. He claimed to have a marketing job, which he did remotely.

When he was an assistant to the Yogi, Maharishi Mahesh, he taught Transcendental Meditation (TM). When that relationship ended, according to this false prophet, he developed an even more effective way of teaching meditation. His dream (or I should say his illusion) was to be on stage teaching his method of meditation to huge groups of people. That's right, he saw himself as another Deepak Chopra or Yogi master.

The problem was he never did the work. Worst of all, after I introduced him to contacts where he could set up group meditation sessions, he never followed through. Revealing the truth to my friends and colleagues, after I had convinced them that he was a trustworthy and gifted person, was embarrassing and humbling. I believed in him too.

When you request from spirit, be precise and ask exactly for what you want. In this case, it was four years after my divorce, and I was lonely and still in search of that unconditional love. I requested a like-minded partner, a man who understood how important meditation was. At that time, I equated meditation with being spiritual. That's when the false prophet appeared in my life.

I forgot to specify that I wanted a truthful, determined, healthy man who had good, elevated energy. In reality, I got what I asked for: A man who meditated but was not a spiritual person. Over the seven months he lived with me, I discovered he had several years of unpaid taxes to the IRS. His car was repossessed for nonpayment, he lost his only two clients from marketing, he needed glasses, had bad teeth, and was an insulin-dependent diabetic.

In addition, when we first connected, he asked a friend, one of his past students, to create an astrology chart for me. She told me that this man and I had been together in many past lifetimes and were destined to be together again. She said we were meant for each other and shared the same goals in life.

Sadly, he had fed her all the information—things I wanted to hear. It worked, hook, line, and sinker. This situation reminded me of a book I read, *Getting Naked Again,* by Judith Sills. The book focuses on dating, sex, and romance when you've been divorced, widowed, dumped, or distracted. One of the chapters I wish I had read more closely was, "Do you want to be a nurse or a purse?" In this situation, I was both. Guess I didn't do my due diligence.

The only good thing about this relationship was that he was adamant about meditating for twenty minutes twice a day. This helped me establish a routine and discipline that I follow today. The relationship ended as soon as I found my voice and sent him packing to live with friends in California.

TWENTY-ONE

INDIANA AND MIKE

Don't waste beautiful time chasing perfection.

While planning a trip to Thailand to complete my Qigong studies at Grandmaster Chia's compound, my plans came to a screeching halt when an old flame reached out to me. Once again, I let my dreams fade away while searching for true love. That was husband number four.

After thirty-five years with no communication, Mike reached out to me on Facebook. At that time, I was content with my lifestyle. I practiced Qigong three times a week, walked two miles on the beach most mornings, led sisterhood groups, hosted a weekly group of mah-jongg, and continued my daily meditation practices.

I was not interested in a serious relationship. After trying several different dating sites, the lies and deceit were just too much. I vowed to be off these sites, and if the universe sent me someone, so be it. When I was looking for my prince, all I found were toads. Still, something was missing from my life. Being lonely and desiring someone to travel and share experiences with drew me toward Mike.

I had known Mike years earlier when I was twenty-eight. He was four years younger. We were in the same water ski club and connected a few times. Two years past my master's program, I had accepted a job in Binghamton, New York to establish a hospital-based speech-language program. There was no time for love relationships in my life. We both went our separate ways.

After Mike visited me in 2016, he sent me cards every week. He wrote poems for me and sent song lyrics that reflected how he felt. On one of his early visits, not trusting my judgment, I introduced Mike to several of my friends to get their feedback. It was a go from everyone. He was a very likable guy. One time he wrote, "I may not be your prince, but I know I won't be a toad."

We grew closer through texts and phone calls. After several visits, I rented an apartment in Indiana to test the waters. After three failed marriages, I needed to be cautious. Was I repeating my mistakes?

His job of wooing me was successful. We were married in January of 2017 on a sailboat in the Florida Keys. The brilliant red ball of sun slid into the ocean as we said our vows. The seven-mile bridge was a magnificent backdrop.

Mike's two grown kids were flown in for the long weekend. My brother, who was already vacationing in the Keys, represented my side of the family. It was a fun celebration. We swam with the dolphins at the Dolphin Research Center, walked on the beach, and ended the celebrations with a full day in Key West.

From the beginning, Mike supported my spiritual journey and activities. He never judged me and occasionally asked how my meditations were going. I never pressured him to join in, and he never asked to accompany me. We spent the early years of our marriage attending musical concerts, cruising, and enjoying many water activities. I was excited to get back into one of my loves, water skiing, which I learned at the age of five. I bought a paddleboard which I used as often as weather permitted.

Mike bought me new ski equipment and I bought a new ski boat for us. We lived on a lake that his family had built years earlier and then erected homes around the perimeter. Before long, I was running the slalom course and entering competitions. Whenever Mike left for trips, he always left me cards showing his love. I would hide little love notes in his luggage. Life was good.

For the first time in my life, I was me. With Mike, I didn't have to chase love. He often reached over and pinched me and said, "I just want to make sure this is real. I dreamed of being with you so many times over the years. I want to make sure that I'm not dreaming now."

Mike was only a couple of inches taller than me and had broad shoulders and muscular arms. We were a perfect fit. I felt safe and peaceful when he held me in his strong arms. It was love, even if it was fleeting.

After retiring from the Postal Service, Mike bought a water treatment business that required him to work and travel from mid-April to the first of November. That seemed to solve the problem of where to live. We compromised and, much to my dismay, became snowbirds. Summers in Florida were one of my favorite times. Traffic improved as did the attitude of the locals. Everything slowed down, beaches were almost empty, restaurant reservations were not necessary, and very few cars honked as the traffic lights turned green.

Spending summers in southern Indiana and winters in Florida was a big sacrifice for me and, I suppose, for Mike as well. Isn't marriage about give and take?

Each day, Mike fell asleep around 7:00 p.m. and woke up around 5:00 a.m. This was his schedule when he worked over forty years at the post office, and his body would not readjust. I woke up around 7:30, took my coffee back to the bed, and meditated. By the time I got up and out of bed for the day, Mike had been up for so long, he was ready for a nap.

Eventually, my morning meditations were on hold so I could rise from bed earlier, have coffee, and chat with my husband. I had every intention to meditate later that day. That good intention faded away with time. I was only listening to unguided meditations at night which lured me to sleep. That was not meditating. As time went on, due to our restless nights and my snoring, Mike started sleeping in the other bedroom. Our time spent together had grown shorter. By that time, I was out of practice with meditations.

I spent my time paddleboarding and reading. The house where we lived had been his parents' home. It was in good shape but outdated. Our plans to update and remodel the inside never happened. Mike was good about starting projects, but not so good at finishing them.

Since there were no flowers or beautiful landscaping on this big piece of land, with joy, I designed and planted a Zen Garden. It was filled with plants and flowers to attract butterflies and other pollinators. I started a vegetable garden and created various other colorful planting areas. These gardens helped to fill my days. A comfortable teak bench under a sprawling maple tree was just the spot for watching the action in my garden.

One day, when walking down the hill with my morning coffee to enjoy the garden, I saw a bald eagle sitting at the very top of what I called the Zen Tree. I was in awe, seeing this mighty creature thought to be the messenger of the Gods by the Native Americans; it stopped me in my tracks.

Spotting an Eagle reminds us to step out of our comfort zone. Find balance in your life, rise above your struggles, and soar to new heights. The Eagle represents strength and security, which allow us to face our fears and keep flying forward. I didn't grasp that it was a message for me.

Upon arriving in Indiana, I immediately searched the area for meditation groups, Qigong practices, or any type of spiritual activity. In a Bible-belting town such as Evansville, filled with churches on every corner, spiritualism outside of the church was taboo. I was still writing in my journal, but spending more and more time alone, since Mike's work frequently took him out of town three to five days a week.

Since I couldn't find any spiritual groups, I thought I'd start my own. Over the six years of marriage in Indiana, I organized only three sisterhood gatherings. Except for the winter solstice celebration, which I held in our dark basement with a roaring fire and candles to honor the light, the other two meetings were a flop. Usually, participants joined in discussions and interacted with each other.

Maybe it was their strict Catholic upbringing that made them uncomfortable, or the Mandela I created with beautiful flowers and candles in the center of the room. Whatever the reason, they gave me one-word answers to the topics I presented.

All my planned activities for the two-hour meeting were completed in the first fifteen minutes. *What the hell am I going to do now?* I quickly dug down in my bag of tricks for another activity. Nothing worked with this group. I was hoping that the ladies would enjoy this gathering and invite their friends the next time.

One of the meetings was in my stepdaughter's house. She was in her late twenties, lacked self-confidence, and was struggling with relationships and her purpose in life. From the first time I met Mike's daughter, he encouraged me to create a bond with her. He felt my positivity and spiritual practices would be a good influence on her life.

One of my goals was to teach his daughter how to conduct these sisterhood gatherings when I was in Florida for the winter. When I am preparing to present a topic, I gain so much knowledge by researching and preparing for each of the group meetings. Since she had expressed an interest in new-age methods, I believed this would create a path for her to learn and follow.

To strengthen our bond, I organized outings for us. We went to the only new-age store in the area. Once a month the store, Treasures and Pleasures, sponsored tarot readings given by an astrologer. My stepdaughter seemed intrigued by this activity.

We attended the exhibit of her favorite artist, Salvador Dali, at the local museum. We went to local nurseries to buy flowers and plants for her yard, and we took hikes in the forest. After finding out she was pregnant, I was very excited about being a grandmother since I had no children of my own. I bought everything this girl wanted for her shower. I painted the baby's nursery. I bought her special food when she found out she had pre-eclampsia. When she arrived home with her baby, I had a Crock-Pot full of roast and veggies waiting for her and her partner.

From the beginning, I remained open and repeatedly told my step-daughter that I wasn't there to replace her mother or to be her best friend. I wanted to be someone special in her life. Someone she could trust.

TWENTY-TWO

MY DISORDER

The tragedy of life is not death but what we let die inside of us while we live.

In 2020, after I had back-fusion surgery, Mike and I moved from my two-bedroom condo in Delray Beach to a four-bedroom house in Winter Haven on beautiful Lake Daisy. Moving to Winter Haven, Florida, the water ski capital of the world, was a dream come true.

My family spent many Christmas breaks in Florida. We always stopped in this quiet little town to visit Cypress Gardens and Bok Singing Towers, before heading down to the Keys.

Sometimes, Dad would launch his boat, and we would travel through the canals connecting the Chain of Lakes in Winter Haven. My family was in awe of this beautiful city surrounded by water and citrus. Moving here was bittersweet, knowing that my father would have loved to be here with me.

That following summer, back in Indiana, I began to feel sick. My loss of appetite, morning nausea, and dry heaves which sometimes lasted all day, resulted in a loss of seventeen pounds. Weighing eighty-seven pounds, I didn't have much energy for anything. I spent most of that summer in bed watching other families have fun on the lake while I just wanted to die. My attempts at meditation were futile. We trust that our bodies will heal themselves with rest and good nutrition. However, my pain and the mystery of my disorder eroded that trust.

Since my Florida doctor retired, and I had not established a doctor in Indiana or Winter Haven, I was left with visits to the emergency room or urgent care units to seek treatment. I had test after test with no conclusions, and the removal of my gallbladder, which turned out to be normal. The first gastroenterologist I saw said, "We may never know for sure what is causing your problem."

Finally, the catch-all term IBS-C (Irritable Bowel Syndrome with Chronic Constipation) was attached to my file. After no help from the current doctors, I sought out a functional physician in Owensboro, Kentucky. On our first meeting, she said, "Deb, if you don't get your mind, body, and soul balanced and aligned, you will die soon."

That scared me, but I knew she was correct. She ordered blood work, including hormone studies, and started me on supplements. She also suggested counseling to help with the anxiety and stress that was making my condition worse. I saw a counselor twice a week for about a month. I returned to morning meditations with deep breathing when the pain in my colon allowed.

TWENTY-THREE

TOXICITY

Light will return, even after the darkest days.

T oward the end of the summer, a toxic situation occurred with Mike's daughter. She had just given birth to a baby girl, Mike's first grandchild. Needless to say, we were both ecstatic. It didn't take long for my dreams of being a grandmother to be squashed. Not only was Mike's daughter not interested in leading any spiritual groups but, two weeks after having the baby, she made it clear that I was not welcome in her new life with the baby.

She sent a lengthy venomous text to me and her father listing all of her dislikes and bothers concerning me. It was silly things, such as I rolled my eyes at her, or I forced my diet on her, or she didn't understand why I had to take her father away to Florida for six months. She had asked me this before, and I explained that, to be a legal citizen of Florida(which her Dad had chosen), the law states that you must live in the state for six months plus a day.

I offered to go to mediation in a neutral setting with a neutral person. She refused to meet with me and discuss her issues, making the entire environment tense. When my integrity is questioned, it hurts to the core. Nothing changed. She believed what she did and refused to speak to me.

I was flabbergasted. This young lady that I had accepted into my life, shared experiences with, and opened up my heart to was now someone who didn't even want to be around me. Looking back over those past years, I realized I had been the one who initiated activities, not her. It always seemed awkward and strained to do things with her. I honestly did not realize that she didn't want to be with me. *How could I be so blind, again?*

My mind was searching for a reason. Had she been resentful or jealous of me? How long had she been harboring these dislikes? Our relationship completely dissolved soon after that, with her blocking me on all media. She refused to meet or accept any of my letters. She sent a message via her father that I would never be welcome in her home or at any birthday celebrations or holidays. Her older brother, who had just opened up a brewery, also sent a message that I was not welcome in his establishment.

Ten years earlier, I could have stood up to this situation and ignored this childish behavior. After all, I married her father, not his two grown children. Now, my health was failing, and my energy was low. Making matters worse, my husband refused to speak to his daughter in my defense. Even when she was spewing lies in front of him, instead of stopping her and correcting her, he sat in silence.

This complicated situation loomed over me. My health issues worsened with no relief. It was obvious to me that stress and anxiety were a serious trigger for my condition. I cried one minute and screamed the next. A nervous breakdown was heading my way, and I was out of control. I was at my lowest, so sick, hurting physically and emotionally, not knowing what was wrong. Every morning waking with nausea that stayed just on the edge most of the day was no way to live.

The day the scales read eighty-six pounds I was sure I was dying. My heart pounded as the vibrations rattled through my thin skin and bones. My clothes were falling off my frail body, my thin face was drawn and wrinkled, with dark circles under my eyes. *Who is that looking back at me in the mirror?* I finally was so disgusted with my looks, that I got pretty good at catching a quick overall glance in the mirror, instead of staring at my face.

I became so depressed with no solution to my situation, that I wrote three separate suicide notes—one to my family, one to my best friend, and another to Mike. During one of my darkest moments, Mike called my best friend, Teresa. I refused to talk to her, but she wouldn't hang up. Her insistent screaming across the phone finally made me take the call. She knew exactly what I needed to hear and calmed me down. Forever friends like this come around once in a lifetime.

My continued request for Mike to emotionally support me and speak to his daughter about these lies was unmet. He just shrugged, stating he wasn't going to put any pressure on her since she was a new mother. He explained that all his life he'd protected her, and he couldn't stop now.

With my condition worsening, I knew I had to get help. The only solution I could see was to remove myself from this toxic situation. Always being one for a challenge, I was determined to find a way to improve my situation. The work had to be done by me. I had to dig deep and find the energy to do what I needed. I had to change my environment before I could think about improving my health. That's when I packed boxes and returned to my home in Winter Haven.

When I needed my husband the most, he abandoned me, emotionally and physically. Instead of protecting me and defending me, he did nothing to prevent this poisonous situation from growing worse.

I stood by my marriage vows. I nursed Mike back to health through four knee operations that required two intravenous daily antibiotics followed by weeks of rehab. I withstood the rough waters as well as the smooth sailing. Mike was not able to navigate these stormy waters. He gave up on us. Supporting his daughter and her beliefs was more important to him than our marriage.

One of the last things Mike said to me was, "I will never put anyone before my children. I would take a bullet for them." Where was I on his totem pole of love? Why did I have to be pushed to the bottom? If the grandchildren kept coming, would there even be room for me?

When speaking of self-love, I heard someone say, "Put yourself at the top of your list, 'cause you are not at the top of anyone else's list."

I certainly wasn't ever going to be the first person on Mike's list. Too late, I realized we were on different paths. Once again, I'd jumped off the cliff without looking. Patience was not one of my virtues. Mike had always been close to his entire family of five siblings, many nieces, nephews, and cousins. My family was spread out in several states. We were lucky to see each other once a year. Mike's family celebrated every holiday and many birthdays together.

In the beginning, these family gatherings were special, something I had never experienced. Mike's extended family were friendly and welcomed me into their lives with love. That wasn't enough. I needed spiritual activities. I needed peace and tranquility to heal.

The situation with his daughter gave me the push to leave. Knowing how close Mike was to his family, how could I possibly continue with this relationship, when I knew he wanted to be a part of his granddaughter's life? I refused to be an obstacle in Mike's life when it came to his family, especially his grandchildren.

After a year of separation with no changes in my husband's attitude, I filed for divorce. At seventy-one, I was divorced and took back my maiden name, Crutcher, vowing to never change it again. Our marriage of six years was over.

Needless to say, my search for unconditional love was unfulfilled with this man. That feeling of failure in my fourth marriage opened the door for emptiness and darkness to creep in. There was still a sense that something was missing in my life. I needed to awaken from the idea of pleasing others or using tangible items to fill the gap within.

TWENTY-FOUR

RETURN TO FLORIDA

Brave birds still fly in fog.

As soon as I returned to Florida, I became established with a doctor who understood my condition and, with his referrals, aided in discovering the cause of my disorder and its treatment. In June of 2023, following a colonoscopy, I received a diagnosis of a redundant tortuous colon with chronic constipation. It's a genetic factor. It means that my colon is too large for my body, which causes turns, twists, and narrowing that interfere with digestion and daily bowel movements.

Side effects are nausea, cramping, colon pain, and chronic constipation. There is no cure, but it won't kill me. It sure does mess with all aspects of my life. Most celebrations and holidays revolve around food. Socializing is difficult, not knowing how your colon will react. Who wants to party with a group who are drinking while you are stone sober? With my unpredictable gut issues, many anxieties surfaced – fear of eating at restaurants, traveling overnight, and attending social gatherings.

I had discussed this condition with all previous doctors, stating that I had a lifetime difficulty with constipation. No one heard me. In the eighth grade, standing outside the school bus that was going to take us on our graduation trip to Saint Louis, I suddenly had a sharp colon pain that nearly dropped me to the ground. Standing straight was out of the question. My father quickly picked me up and carried me to the car, stating that I was not going on this trip. I was devasted at missing the trip and humiliated that all my classmates were looking on. Begging my father to let me go was useless.

When we arrived home, I pleaded with my mother not to discuss my embarrassing situation with any of her friends or neighbors. The next Monday, when I arrived at school, my class sang this little ditty: "Debbie couldn't go on the class trip, because she was full of shit."

My mother had told the neighbor, who told her son, who was a year younger than me and couldn't keep a secret any more than our moms could. The day I confronted my mother about this, I vowed in silence to never trust her again. As a sensitive child, I was too shy to stand up to the bullies in my class. I hadn't found my voice. I didn't even know I was supposed to have one.

TWENTY-FIVE

CONFRONTING THE DIAGNOSIS

Are you willing to wait for the mud to settle
and the water to clear?

S ettled back in my Florida home with my new diagnosis, I began
the arduous task of discovering what foods I could ingest and
what foods were triggers. The fact that I didn't know how certain
items influenced my digestion until the next day made this task more

complicated. Sometimes the unpleasantness and pain from eating the wrong thing lasted for days.

The fear of food was not helpful with my goal of gaining weight while maintaining good nutrition. Permanently eliminating certain foods and alcohol from my diet was a necessity for my health. Drinking homemade smoothies twice a day with ingredients such as avocado, spinach, fresh fruit, flax seed, and protein powder based in coconut water and pomegranate juice kept me alive. This drink continues to be part of my daily routine.

When I resumed my morning meditations, my monkey mind was having difficulty focusing. My scattered thoughts were bouncing from one to another. I tried and tried, but I couldn't get to that quiet place. Looking inward to remove obstacles was momentary. I had moments of bliss, but I couldn't hang on to the feeling of peace and tranquility throughout my day.

That's why it's called a meditation "practice." With any activity, if you don't stay with it, you lose some of the sharpness. Deep darkness was still locked away, but it was getting full and starting to seep out little by little, contaminating my soul and my mind. I needed to slow down and be patient—an attribute I'm not too familiar with. I always have this tendency to want everything now, instant gratification. Spirituality doesn't work like that. Time to go back to peeling the layers of the onion.

In Florida, it was easier to find like-minded people and activities that aligned with my path than in Indiana. I discovered sound baths at Bok Tower, where the leader played beautiful crystal and copper bowls to decrease anxiety and stress while promoting relaxation.

The leader, Anthony Profeta, is a former medical student. He became disillusioned by the medical field when he found out that most of our diseases and disorders are caused by anxiety and stress. Yet, in his medical training, techniques to decrease anxiety and stress to improve a patient's health were never addressed. Too often a pharmaceutical path of painkillers was recommended.

Retreating from the medical field, Anthony turned to teaching meditation and mindfulness after spending years studying with various masters, including the Dalai Lama. He sponsors healing sessions and retreats all over the world.

TWENTY-SIX

MOON DREAMZ

The universe hears what you feel, not what you say.

While I struggled to meditate, the universe listened to my request for guidance. One day, while at Home Depot, I asked an employee where a certain item was. She commented on the beautiful Larimar stone I was wearing. We started talking about crystals, and she reached into her pocket, pulled out several, and said "I'm never without mine." It was a fortunate stroke of serendipity to meet someone while shopping who not only knew about crystals but ultimately led me to Moon Dreamz, a metaphysical store, in the same town where I lived. As we talked a bit, she said she was a Reiki master and that she and several others would be providing Reiki healing that week at Moon Dreamz.

Reiki is a safe, gentle technique that uses spiritual energy to treat ailments without pressure or massage. Energy is channeled through to the body to clear unwanted patterns and to enhance the balance of mind, body, and spirit. If successful, Reiki results in a deep sense of peace.

When I arrived that Friday evening at Moon Dreamz for the session, I was elated when I saw a list of activities that aligned with my spiritual goals. The store sponsored crystal workshops, drum circles, inner child workshops, celebrations of the solstice, tarot readings, and much more. Following the Reiki session, I scheduled my first past-life regression session with one of their employees, which was amazing. Moon Dreamz continued to be one of the places I attended regularly.

TWENTY-SEVEN

FINDING MY GURU AND MY TRIBE

The teacher will appear when the student is ready.

Some people are only meant to be in your life for a short while for a specific reason or lesson; others are there for longer. Another example that the universe sent me what I needed was when I was introduced to Miss Quinn's spiritual group.

A friend forwarded information she had seen on Facebook about a group of ladies who met in the nearby woods. The woods, which were owned and maintained by the Audubon Society were right around the corner from where I lived. It was one of my favorite places to walk among the shady, moss-ridden massive trees. Mulched pathways led through this cornucopia of nature, wildflowers, and birds. Since the group met in the evenings, I'd never seen them on my morning walks.

After contacting the group leader, Sharon Quinn, on Facebook and getting permission to attend, on June 14, 2023 I walked to the woods for my first session with a bit of skepticism. Six of us women lay or sat on our yoga mats in a clearing in the woods under a giant arch made by a fallen branch.

Sharon didn't look like I expected. She was in her late forties with beautiful golden hair hanging down her back, bright blue eyes, and glowing skin. She was from Leicester, United Kingdom. I learned that, earlier in her life, she had modeled for Christian Dior, Neiman Marcus, and other agencies which took her all over the world. Sharon acted on a couple of episodes of the television show, *Baywatch*, and later was a TV producer in Miami for the show, *Top Surgeons*.

She was going through a tough divorce and had two young girls. She was born with this spiritual gift but did not develop or train until later in her life.

Unfortunately, when children hear voices and see images or have an imaginary friend, most adults move quickly to diminish those experiences, instead of helping to develop their gift. Sharon's gift was silenced, or at least they tried. She eventually attended workshops in England at Leicester Progressive Spiritual Church with teachers who recognized her gift.

As the energy from the woods washed over me at that first gathering, Sharon played her colorful crystal bowls sending vibrational waves throughout my body. She walked among us and played various instruments—a glass crystal pyramid, a harp tuned to 440 Hz frequency,

African rattles, tuning forks, rain sticks, or one of her many drums, while she guided us through a meditation.

She made a couple of personal comments that struck home with me, things she wouldn't have known. I had never met her or talked to her. *How did she know these things?* That wasn't the last time Sharon surprised me with personal information. After that first gathering, I wanted to run away. *What was I getting into? Who was this lady and how did she know personal information about me? Was she gifted, or was this just an opportunity for her?* I decided to visit the group a few more times before forming an opinion.

I found myself drawn to the group as if Sharon was sent to guide me on my journey. I soon discovered that she was the "real deal." I have had readings from several people in different locations, palm readings, astrology charts created, and sound baths from various leaders, but nothing compared to Sharon's gifts.

One word to describe Sharon is not possible, for she is so much more. Source channels through her providing messages that are accurate and profound. She has used her gift to help find lost items or lost people. Her energy is phenomenal and strong. Spirit engulfs her. It's impossible to be around her and not be affected by her enthusiasm and love of spirituality.

I continued the weekly sisterhood meetings and became more comfortable. Each meeting was a little different, depending on who showed up and the energy present. Coming out of our meditations, we shared our experiences and discussed anything we wanted to release. I left these sessions feeling relaxed and peaceful. Sharon has a gift of holding space and keeping the energy of our meetings centered, grounded, and filled with peace, love, and gratitude. I had found my tribe, a place of belonging, a safe place to share my voice with my sisters.

They say when you meditate one day alone, it is a great thing. When you meditate in a group, it is like meditating seven days in a row. There's a connection, an unspoken camaraderie among us. These groups are infused with kindness, compassion, and love. Our weekly mediations with Sharon are more deeply rooted because we are among nature. We almost always hear the call of an owl at dusk or see a hawk flying into the woods to roost. At times, Sharon leads us to walk with gratitude and intention through the woods as we drum to the beat of Mother Earth.

Once a month, I scheduled one-on-one sessions with Sharon, which were more intense than the group meetings. That locked compartment in my gut was pretty full, and some unpleasant emotions and memories were surfacing. Through these individual sessions, I discovered and purged regrets, anger, shame, disappointments, and mistakes from my past which were impeding my forward movement.

During some of the sessions, I screamed and cried as I released the unnecessary demons. This is called "Shadow Work." By releasing these unwanted emotions, I became more self-aware of my feelings and looked at myself from a different perspective. As stated before, purging negativity makes room for more love.

The universe, once again, provided exactly what I needed, what I asked for. Sharon Quinn not only became my gifted guru, but a trusted friend. I believe a person can raise their vibration and improve their spirituality alone. Somewhere along the way, finding someone to guide you is necessary for your growth. Much like trying to fold a bed sheet, it is so much easier with someone to help you. She continues to provide guidance for me and answer the multitude of questions I have along the road.

As time went on, I came forward to volunteer my assistance in receiving participants, collecting money, smudging, adding decoration, or whatever else was necessary. I discovered there were several ladies in desperate need of healing but didn't have the funds. Sharon still welcomed them into the group.

Sharon's goal to open her spiritual healing sanctuary will soon be a reality. I know it will be a great success and, more importantly, will benefit so many people who are lost or hurt and trying to find which road to take on their journey. My work with Miss Sharon Quinn will continue until my last days.

TWENTY-EIGHT

MANIFESTING

Where your attention goes, energy will flow.

Thinking back on my spiritual journey, it seemed the more I learned, the more I realized I didn't know. Spiritualism doesn't happen in an instant. It's not like the Southern Baptist revivals where someone (a so-called sinner) walked forward, repented, and was saved on the spot. Spirituality was all around me, but I was barely waking up.

While participating in the Artist Way workshop, one of the students who was a lawyer talked about manifesting her business to create more abundance. She discussed how she placed the amount of salary she wanted for the next year above her work area and repeated it every day. *At first, I thought, really? She just asked for it and it happened. What? How could this be?*

In the end, she was successful. This was a good example of how positive thoughts bring positive actions.

I was reluctant at the time to ask questions since I didn't want to appear the novice that I was. The other members seemed to know so much about visualization, manifesting, and self-love. I did what I was good at: I observed, listened, took mental notes, then researched a topic and learned more about it. Years later, I understood what manifesting was and can testify that it works.

Deepak Chopra suggested writing, at least once a month, exactly what you really, really, really want in your life. I wrote things that most people want, like peace, tranquility, travel, good health, beautiful flowers, good books, and happiness. Writing it down is good to set your intentions, but manifesting is much more.

To manifest what you want, you must visualize it, feel it, and know it to be true. In one of my groups, one of the ladies wanted to find her soulmate. She manifested this desire daily. She finally placed a pair of men's shoes by the door, so she would know how it felt to come home to her man. I left that group before finding out if her desires were answered.

After the divorce from Mike, I needed to downsize from a lakeside four-bedroom three-bath home with a large yard, which I could no longer maintain. For six months I wrote every week, "I want a two-bedroom, two-bath condo with an attached garage and a lake view, in the community of Winterset." Each time I wrote that sentence, I visualized myself sitting in the screened lanai, feeling the breeze from the lake, and imagining the view of a sunset or a full moon rising. I felt peace and tranquility.

Every week, this practice was repeated, while viewing any condo that would appear on the market in that area. After three failed offers, the exact unit I wanted was available. At the same time, I had a great offer on my house. Everything fell into place.

It's important, once you've manifested your intention, to believe it, own it, then give it to the universe. Deepak called this "The Law of Detachment." When you let go of control, you tend to attract even more of what you desire.

Manifesting isn't about getting, it's about allowing. It's about receiving what is of the highest good for you. If you forge ahead with blinders on, you may miss other possibilities that the universe has in mind for you. When you align your frequency with what you want, and you feel it, the universe will support you.

Manifesting is the idea that your positive thoughts, and the power of belief and feeling, will develop into reality. We are all energy. When our energy is low, we attract low-vibrational situations and people. On the other hand, when we vibrate at a higher frequency, we attract positive outcomes and people radiating at our energy level.

When I sit on my lanai with my purring cat at my feet and view the crimson sunset over the lake or sit outside late at night in silence waiting for the moon to rise, I feel tranquility and peace. I am grateful and blessed. I received exactly what I manifested. The universe took care of the details.

TWENTY-NINE

LEARNING LESSONS

One of the most difficult things in life is deciding which bridge to cross and which to burn.

L earning lessons was a long process for me. Finding an authentic spiritual leader, such as Sharon, kept me on the right path. Each unpleasant issue I had locked away had to be dealt with. A counselor told me that once you finally learn a lesson, there'll be another one thrown at your feet. Until I was in my seventies, I didn't understand what it meant to learn a lesson.

After getting out of a bad situation I would say, "Well, I've learned that lesson. I won't do that again." Had I learned a lesson, or was I feeling anger, humility, shame, or resentment? Is that the reason I pushed it down and sealed it away?

Ask yourself, what was your reaction in that situation? Why did you feel like that? Can you look at it with love? What was your lesson in this situation? Only then can you release. You don't need that memory eating away at your soul.

Cleanse away negativity and invite love and healing into your life. Accept this life lesson, stop looking backward, and walk into the now.

Recognizing those feelings, allowing them to drift to the top, and dealing with them must be accomplished to move forward. Releasing the past can be messy and painful, but it's the only way. Walk into the flames and let go. When we learn the lessons, we can move forward.

There will always be light and dark in our lives. The goal is to recognize the positive and negative but to gently neutralize the darkness, so it does not harm. Be in tune with your body so you can grab and control the dark dog before it bites you.

THIRTY

THE FIGHT BETWEEN CHRONIC PAIN AND SELF-LOVE

"Love is more than a romantic partnership. Embrace the power of your unique gifts. Divine love is within." ...
Dalai Lama

When you are dealing with deep chronic pain, striving for self-love is complicated. Focusing on your practice takes extreme determination and concentration. I love who I am at my core––my morality, honesty, loyalty, compassion, and thirst for knowledge. I'm proud of all my accomplishments. I am grateful to have experienced many things in my lifetime. However, none of that was important when I was in pain and struggling.

I don't love what my body is doing. I don't love the pain, the discomfort and especially how it disrupts and interferes with this last season of my life. One of the worst things about my condition is that it is invisible.

I used to think that I had to lead with my disorder when I met someone new. It was easier to explain why I don't go out to bars drinking or why I don't eat at most restaurants, since my diet is so limited.

Some mornings when I woke up with nausea and the feeling that a huge stone was sitting in my colon, or a flare-up kept me in bed most of the day, I would ask, Is this it? Is the best of my life over? I had my chance to enjoy life, and I blew it. Now deterioration and loss are on the fast track, and I can't stop it. How do I continue with self-love when there are parts of me that I don't love?

We are trained to believe we can handle life's challenges and learn our lessons. However chronic pain, like I have, eats away at that belief. We want to push through with determination, but pain distracts and holds us back. When pain robs us of socialization, experiences, family, and relationships, the darkness creeps in pretty fast.

There is no such thing as a pain-free life. There's always some sort of pain in our lifetime. Karim Rushdy, a teacher of mindfulness, states, "Pain is inevitable; suffering is optional." His ten-day course on "Unpacking Pain and Stress with Mindfulness" can be found on the app Insight Timer.

Rushdy says, "Free the mind and let go of emotions. That way you can discover where the root of your behavior lies." His course advises on accepting and relating to the pain which promotes negative thinking. Shedding the negative emotions swirling around the pain is necessary to move on.

It is a challenge to meditate when I am in pain. Deep breathing, a heating pad, and massaging around my stomach and colon usually help me. The focused breathing calms my anxiety and makes the pain seem less emotionally burdensome. If not, I find another time in the day that is better.

My digestive disorder, redundant tortuous colon which has no cure, prevents me from using any type of pain medication, not even an aspirin. So many medications have a side effect of constipation, which I must avoid. I have found cannabis products to be the most effective in dealing with my insomnia, pain, and morning nausea. I use a transdermal gel with THC and CBD for my pain and an RSO cannabis sub-lingual tincture at night for pain and sleep. If the nausea turns into dry heaves, a couple of hits of ground flower gives instant relief.

Cannabis research is surfacing out of the dark. More and more products are being developed utilizing different terpenes of the marijuana plant. It is a welcome replacement for heavy, addictive narcotic painkillers.

THIRTY-ONE

SELF-LOVE

Open your heart to yourself. Love, accept, embrace,
celebrate you.

Dealing with complications of aging compounded the situation of self-love for me. Menopause drained the life out of my hair and body, leaving a desert where soft, supple skin and shiny hair once were. Insomnia set in, and my woman parts atrophied and dried up like an old well that hasn't been used in years.

Self-love was difficult for this aging woman as I was determined to continue on my spiritual journey. Along my way, aches and pains were a daily occurrence. Bit by bit I gave up activities as my mind said, "Yes," but my body said, "I don't think so." These changes were depressing. Commitments were difficult since I never knew how my body was going to react. It was a grieving process, and I slowly let go as parts of my body failed me. Because of my arthritic back and sciatic pain, I could no longer dance, paddleboard, or water ski. Traveling and going out to eat were put on hold.

The media makes it more complicated by giving us messages that we are not good enough. We need to be thin, fit, have shiny long hair, and dress fashionably. Society wants us to add things to our life, tempting us with new diets and medications, new cars, or new homes.

It is easy to get caught up in the propaganda that something is wrong with you. However, the release of things no longer needed is powerful. With the shedding of layers, you start to become who you truly are, and you rise above. There are still bad days as that emotional roller coaster takes a dip, but now you don't go as deep, and you bounce back faster to your spiritual routine.

I compare it to one of my favorite childhood stories, *The Velveteen Rabbit*. Through years of love, the little rabbit went through changes. The little rabbit said, "You become. It takes a long time. That's why it doesn't happen often to people who break easily or have sharp edges, or who have to be carefully kept. Generally, by the time you are Real, most of your hair has been loved off, and your eyes drop out and you get loose in the joints and very shabby. But these things don't matter at all, because once you are Real you can't be ugly, except to people who don't understand."

We don't know where we will be in five, ten, twenty years from now. As we age, sickness and death circle close by as we lose friends and loved ones. Time seems to be rushing by. Think of all the changes our body goes through beginning with our first breath—crawling, walking, first day of school. Our hormones kick in, hair appears in new places, we grow taller, and we bleed.

Remember when you thought you were never going to reach sixteen so you could get your driver's license? Or to be twenty-one and legal for that drink? Every milestone is a celebration. Somewhere along the aging path, we stop celebrating so much. When people say, "I hate birthdays," I say, "It's better than the alternative."

Why not celebrate another year? Your body can still be loved, touched, and caressed. I highly recommend massages to people who live alone and essentially never receive a hug or a loving touch. Embrace your aging markers and your scars; they are testimonies to your life. Shine on from the inside.

In the blink of an eye, my bucket list is staring me in the face. I am trying to figure out which items are unrealistic, such as diving with the humpback whales. And which ones to focus on, such as trips to local beaches, reading poetry one more time at the Key West Poetry Society, and visiting my family. With trepidation, mingled with determination, I am tiptoeing back into traveling.

My concern is figuring out how to accomplish my desires while at the same time tolerating my health issues. I am positive, as I move forward with my consistent routine and working with spirit, that I will enjoy some of my favorite activities again. Going through these difficult times, I am reminded to be close to my source and to increase my meditations with purposeful intentions.

When you have released all that does not serve you from your past and present, and you have a meditation practice established, you must take care of yourself. We--who are the givers, the healers, the empaths, and the nurturers--so often ignore ourselves, while caring for others.

In my work as a speech-language pathologist with stroke victims and head-injury patients, I often saw the caregiver get sick while the injured patient, receiving all the care, improved. We must keep some of the love and care for ourselves.

There is a parable about an elderly man and his sick wife The man devoted his entire time tending to his beloved, providing her food and water. The homeless couple lived in the center of the village under a huge ancient tree. Eventually the woman grew so ill that the village people feared her contamination and asked the couple to leave the village.

They retreated to a cave several miles out of town. The man walked into the village every morning to beg for bread for his wife. As he fed his wife, he took nothing for himself. One morning, the man passed out in the village and died. With no one to care for his wife, soon the woman followed him in death. The moral is: Don't give it all away; keep something for yourself.

Self-love continues to be difficult for me. I detest asking others for help, yet I love to give, to serve. I receive so much more when I give out of love, without expecting anything in return. When I see someone suffering or in need, it triggers an emotion in me to help. I feel the pain in my gut. When I prepare a warm meal for someone sick or give a worker a cool drink, there is love and joy attached.

Why can't I console myself as I help others? Why can't I give myself what I need? The kindness and compassion we have for others must be turned inward as well.

Trying to fix or change my partner was one of my stories. I told myself, "He needs me. How can I leave when he needs my help?"

Throughout my life, several men have left me for other women. Each one told me, "I'm sorry, but she needs me more than you do. You are strong; you will be fine, but she needs me more."

I gave so much to my partners, trying to fill their every need, while ignoring my own. These experiences were frustrating and hurtful.

I wasn't a needy person. I was independent and strong––the opposite of my mother, which was my goal. At the time, I didn't realize my strength was such a threat to men, and that I would end up living alone.

After twenty years of marriage to my third husband, he revealed that he had gotten a young lady pregnant. With tears in his eyes, he said that I, as his wife, should have noticed he had a problem, helped him and saved him. The mother of the twins was a prostitute who worked the streets of Fort Lauderdale. This man had cheated on me throughout our marriage.

During the first years of that marriage, I was on cloud nine. Each year, we traveled to France, where I fell in love with the country, went on live-aboard dive trips throughout the world, and vacationed with our snow ski club in Colorado, Utah, and the European Alps.

This man was a charmer and a master at control. Throughout the years, his true personality was revealed. He was a Dr. Jekyll and Mr. Hyde. I never knew when or why he would erupt in anger. He was verbally abusive, controlling, and demanding.

In the end, when he asked me to help with his addictive sex problem, I recommended a counselor I was currently seeing. Then, I packed my bags. Three lawyers and four years later, I was finally free of this man.

Another quote by The Dalai Lama: "The secret to finding happiness in life is not about money or power. It is about kindness, compassion, honesty, and truth, first for yourself. The love you have for yourself will ripple through everything—your family, friends, nature, Mother Earth, and her animals."

Finally, I understood what Deepak was talking about when he said love was everything. First, love yourself, then turn outward to touch everyone and every living thing.

Buddhism believes that finding enlightenment or inner peace is like building a house. First, prepare the ground, take measurements, and ensure the foundations are solid. Studying and continuing to practice your meditations, grounding, releasing, and manifesting are all ways to solidify your base. It's like peeling an onion layer by layer.

How can we expect others to love us, when we do not love ourselves? So many times, I have looked to others for my happiness. Unfortunately, when your happiness depends on outside influences or your mate, then your joy can disappear when the influences or the people leave your life.

In the British series *Bridgerton*, a wise woman explained to a young debutante, "There is no true love without first embracing your true self."

How do we acquire self-love and practice it consistently? I've heard that all the love you have ever felt is inside you, waiting, observing. We need to look inward, let everything fall away, remove all obstacles so we can touch this love, and let it permeate through our entire body, mind, and soul.

A quote from the poet, Rumi, can be applied to self-love: "Your task is not to seek love, but merely to seek and find all the barriers within yourself that you have built against it and embrace them."

THIRTY-TWO

A SPIRITUAL LIFESTYLE

Why stay in prison when the door is open?

B eing spiritual is a lifestyle, a slow transformation or awakening along the way. Many moments of, "Oh, so that's it," or "Now I understand what that means." Peeling back the layers one by one to reveal the truths. How often have you heard the term "meditation practice"? Because we strive to elevate our energy with every meditation, it takes practice, dedication, and patience.

Most spiritual leaders suggest meditating twice a day for at least twenty minutes. Scientists have proven that whatever we do in the first thirty minutes of our day sets the trajectory for the rest of the day. If we connect to stillness and silence in the morning, we will live with greater ease throughout the day.

There are hundreds of ways to meditate, bridging the physical world with the spiritual. Starting with the twenty-one-day guided meditation from Deepak Chopra and Oprah was an excellent way for me to become disciplined about my daily practice. Using the app, Insight Timer has been wonderful, as they have many recorded meditations.

There are different types of meditation, depending on your intention or how you are feeling. Sometimes, I prefer to meditate to instrumental music, or I have specific guided meditations on the app that I prefer. Some of my favorites are the drumming sessions that take me on a Shamanic journey.

Lately, I have enjoyed sitting in silence and requesting spirit. I have also been practicing forest bathing, which is simply dense woods by a lake. Massive trees and greenery surround me as I breathe in nature's fresh oxygen.

I used to think I was spiritual because I meditated twice a day. I believed in the power of the universe and tried my best to lead a kind and compassionate life. Truth is, I was moving so fast through my days, not aware of the details, as if I was sleepwalking.

Being mindful or spiritual is not just when we meditate. It is a quality of life carried over into our daily activities. When you finish a meditation, take your peace with you throughout your day––that quiet, serene feeling, the energy you received from grounding yourself.

Now that my knowledge and experience have grown as I believe my vibrational energy has elevated, I feel spirituality around me and within me most of the time. I see signs that the spirit is with me. My special number is seventeen. I see this number throughout my day. Many times when I need some encouragement, the number will show up on my watch, on my car clock, or minutes left on a timer. The message could be a cool breeze on a windless day. I slow down and request spirit or one of the Archangels to guide or protect me, as I know they are with me always.

I replaced jealousy with gratitude, negative thoughts and words with positive affirmations, regrets with accomplishments, and sorrow with joy. I am softer and kinder, especially with my words. I think before I spill words that are unkind or unnecessary.

I have learned it's okay if someone is not "right." I don't have to prove it. I don't always have to give my opinion. It's much more beneficial to listen than to talk. Encouraging others to share their feelings and thoughts is my goal.

For me, walking the spiritual path creates a feeling of fullness where emptiness once was; a sense of contentment instead of restlessness; being awake to the world around me, rather than racing through with blinders.

There comes a time on your spiritual journey when you turn your interest to others. It is not all about you all the time. Turn your light outward to shine for others, nature, and the planet.

When I turn my light outwards, I feel an urgency to share my joy and happiness with others—people who need compassion, understanding, and perhaps some guidance. When I help others, my heart is injected with a shot of gratitude and love. As I continue to walk this path for a higher self, I hope to attract relationships that are more positive and aligned with my life goals.

As you seek a higher version of yourself you will separate from those who don't share your beliefs. Most emotionally balanced people are comfortable being alone, with a growing desire to spend *more* time alone, more isolation, and not as many social interactions. This could be your higher self, requesting solitude.

The world I had been living in blended with my spiritual connections. That's a tricky situation to navigate. My desire to be among like-minded people caused me to lose a few others along the way, those who were resistant and negative to my new life-path.

There will always be those who try to control and convince you that their beliefs are for everyone and that their way is the only right direction. I have learned to leave these people with light and love. They do not receive an invitation to join my journey. At this stage, recognizing false prophets, deceit, lies, toxic people and toxic situations is easier to detect. Patience—in the end, the mud will settle, the water will clear, and the truth will rise to the top.

As we connect to source and raise our vibration, we connect with love to nature, animals, and everything around us. Then we connect to like-minded people and build our own family, our tribe. Birds of a feather flock together. You become aware of your ego trying to fill you with fears, worries, regrets, and doubts. But from your higher self, you listen to your intuition, your heart. You have unconditional love and gratitude for others and yourself.

You may find that you move away from certain social activities. Noisy bars and large crowds of people don't interest me anymore. Instead of watching the nightly news and certain violent television shows, I prefer to read, write, or watch a movie I have chosen. Watching a stand-up comic at bedtime puts me in a happy mood for sleep.

Owning my voice and being spiritual means I can speak my truth. I will never be silenced or censored again. I have compassion and care for others as I take care of myself. I can express my boundaries to others without guilt. I feel confident when I say "no" to situations my body cannot handle, such as drinking alcohol, eating at most restaurants, or avoiding stressful people.

Being a female with an authentic voice does not mean I am advocating women's protests or an uprising of women's liberation. I burned my bras in college and had to buy new ones when I started my career. I am one hundred percent for women's rights. We can have our voice, stand up for our rights, and still rejoice in who we are as women.

Knowing and loving yourself will empower you to remove toxic people and places from your life. Remember, if you have to walk the path alone, go forward; your people will find you.

I found my voice and, for the moment, the demons from my past have been released. I've forgiven myself, and I love who I am. The unconditional love I was searching for was inside me, hiding, waiting to be acknowledged. Love fills the emptiness and glows for all.

Is life perfect? No. I still have bad days filled with aging aches and pains and obstacles out of my control. As I was writing this, I spent time with my older brother, who has always been a picture of health, as he was entering the final stages of terminal cancer. The darkness surrounded me as I thought of my mortality and a world without my brother. One thing I realized: Dealing with death puts you in the now, with every breathing moment being precious.

I increased my meditations and requests for spirit to protect and give me clarity. Each morning I acknowledged what I was grateful for. Loving and knowing myself, I didn't travel as far down that dark hole, and I climbed back quicker than before.

My spiritual journey will continue until my day on Earth is finished. I will continue to do the work, meditating, reading, expanding my knowledge, and being mindful of my actions and words.

Ongoing, the work with my spiritual leader, Miss Sharon Quinn, will remain a part of my journey. My wish is that my story and my message will relate to others and aid them in finding and protecting their true voice.

Buddha once said, "This existence of ours is as transient as autumn clouds. To watch the birth and death of beings is like looking at the movements of a dance. A lifetime is like a flash of lightning in the sky, rushing by like a torrent down a steep mountain."

We are stardust, a spark, transient on this planet. Each one of us has a unique gift to share: The ability to love ourselves and everything on Mother Earth.

So, I ask you in the words of the poet laureate, Mary Oliver, "What will you do with your one precious life?"

THIRTY-THREE

RISE, SISTER, RISE

Rise, Sister, Rise
Mothers, Daughters,
sisters worldwide
spread wings
ascend.
Time for Silence
has ended.
Be loud
be brave
be proud.
The moment is now.
Change is upon us.
The world needs
your magic, your gifts,

your unique power.
Dig deep,
flood the dark shadows
with light, hope, and love.
Stand with
determination, confidence.
Let feminine energy
explode from your soul.
Tear down walls that
sheltered fears, and
crushed dreams.
Ignite ancient
wisdom smoldering
in your veins.
Awaken.
Pierce the silence
with your voice.
Rise, Sister, Rise.
Together, we will
sing our song.
By Deb Crutcher

THIRTY-FOUR

POSITIVE AFFIRMATIONS

When I hear a word or phrase that stops me or moves me as I read, listen to music, or watch a movie, I write it down in a small notebook and keep it with me. Some are posted in different places in my home—my journal, fridge, and my purse. They are reminders to keep me centered and focused. You can develop your own list or use the ones below.

*****

- The universe hears what you feel, not what you say.

- Worrying is senseless, like walking around with an umbrella waiting for rain.

- I do not force connections with anyone who does not appreciate my value.

- It's not your job to like me; It's mine. . . . Bryon Katie

- Manipulation is when they blame you for your reaction to their disrespect.

- Don't abandon yourself for the sake of another.

- Never settle for less than the life you deserve.

- You deserve people in your life who don't have misconceptions about your personality or intentions.

- Energy goes where your attention goes.

- Positive thinking brings positive action, and negative thoughts cause negative actions.

- One of the most difficult things in life is deciding which bridge to cross and which to burn . . . . David Russell

- What you seek is seeking you.

- A lifetime is like a flash of lightning in the sky, rushing by like a torrent down a steep mountain. . . . Buddha

- Lock up your libraries, if you like, but there is no lock, no bolt that you can set upon the freedom of my mind. . . . Virginia Woolf

- Wherever you go among the midst of movement and activity, carry your stillness with you. . . . Deepak Chopra

- Why stay in prison, when the door is open?

- Accept it, absorb it, acknowledge it. Bask in the glow.

- Let go of the notion that life has to be hard.

- Step away from emotions that drain.

- Open your heart to receive unlimited love.

- Take your hands off the wheel and coast for a while.

- Unfurl your sail, and drift . . . Let Go.

- Let go of the "If Onlys."

- Know that all is as it should be

- Flow with ease like water. Bloom without a struggle, like a flower.

- Smile to a new day.

- Unfold your wings and discover you could always fly.

- Light will return even after the darkest days.

- We cannot see our reflection in running water—only in still water.

- Are you willing to wait for the mud to settle and the water to clear?

- Eyes, once opened, would not be forced closed again.

- Step out of the darkness of the past and into the light.

- Lift one leg out of the past, step over into the NOW, and soar into the future.

- Don't waste beautiful time chasing perfection.

- Commit to loving yourself.

- Love yourself as the most precious thing in the universe, because you are.

- All I seek is within.

- Brave birds still fly through fog.

- The tragedy of life is not death, but what we let die inside of us while we live.

- The greatest treasure that you will ever find is the light within you.

- As the sunflower turns its face to the light of the sun, so Spiritualism turns the face of humanity to the light of the truth.

- May you always find the light within and have the courage to take a chance.

- You are loved. You are beautiful. You are needed. You are stronger than you think.

- Sometimes the disrespect is all the closure you need.

- Never forget that WALKING AWAY from something un-healthy is BRAVE. Even if you stumble a little on your way out the door.

- The more we give, the more we receive.

- If you want to enter my life, the door is open. If you want to exit my life, the door is open. One request: Please don't stand in the doorway; you're blocking traffic.

- If your happiness comes from within, it is difficult for something on the outside to touch it.

- I will no longer allow the negative things in my life to spoil all the good things I have.

- Life is not a matter of milestones but of moments.

- There will always be a reason why people come into your life. Either you need them to change your life, or you're the one that will change theirs.

- Often when people criticize your life, they are usually the same people who don't know the price you paid to get where you are today.

- Open your heart to yourself. Love, accept, embrace, and celebrate yourself.

- Listen to the wind; it talks. Listen to the silence; it speaks. Listen to your heart; it knows.

SOURCES

Cameron, Julia. *The Artist's Way*, New York, NY: Penguin Putman Inc, 1992.

Banks, Coleman. *Rumi the Book of Love*, New York, NY: Harper-Collins Publishers,2003.

Chia, Mantak. *Awaken Healing Energy Through The Tao*, Santa Fe, New Mexico: Aura Press, 1983.

Chopra, Deepak. *The Seven Spiritual Laws of Success*, New World Library: Amber-Allen Publishing, 1994.

Chopra, Deepak. *The Book of Secrets*, New York: Three Rivers Press, 2004.

Dispenza, Joe, M.D. *Breaking the Habit of Being Yourself*, New York: Hay House, 2012.

Ingram, Sandra. *Walking in Light*, Boulder, Colorado: Sounds True, 2014.

Ingram, Sandra. *The Book of Ceremony*, Boulder, Colorado: Sounds True, 2018.

Insight Timer. https://insighttimer.com

Moon Dreamz Metaphysical supply store. 2750 U.S.-17, Winter Haven, Florida

Oliver, Mary. *House of Light,* Boston Beacon Press, 1992

Oprah and Deepak. *Desire and Destiny,* 21-day meditation experience, Carlsbad, CA: Chopra Center meditation.com, 2013.

Profeta, Anthony. https://anthonyprofeta.com

Quinn, Sharon. www.spiritwithsharonquinn.com

Sills, Judith. *Getting Naked Again,* New York, NY: Springboard Press, 2009.

The Crystal Garden store, 2610 Federal Highway, Boynton Beach, Florida

Tolle, Echart. *The Power of Now: A Guide to Spiritual Enlightenment,* Vancouver, B.C., Canada, 1999.

Williams, Margery. *The Velveteen Rabbit:* Harper Perennial Classics, 2013.

ABOUT THE AUTHOR

Born in Western Kentucky, Deb Crutcher received her master's degree in Speech-Language Pathology from Murray State University. She is a water lover, which explains her favorite activities of paddle boarding, water skiing, swimming, kayaking, and scuba diving.

While living in the Florida Keys, she trained as a volunteer at the Dolphin Research Center, was an active member of the Friends of Old Seven, and published her collection of poems, *Living on the Edge,* which is available on Amazon.

She is a member of the Winter Haven Writers Group, the Authors Mastermind Group, and the Florida Writers Association. Deb mainly writes poetry and creative non-fiction. Much of her work has been published in various anthologies, newspapers, and brochures.

Her thirst for spirituality has spanned many years, which she likens to "Peeling back the layers of an onion to reveal the core." She continues to work on her spirituality with daily meditations, weekly sisterhood groups, and individual sessions with her spiritual leader and friend, Miss Sharon Quinn.

Helping others to gain clarity and to increase their vibrational energy level through her story and guidance is Deb's goal. She desires to have interactive discussions about the roller coaster effects and how to maneuver through life's challenges while maintaining a spiritual life.

Deb and her cat, Zoe, currently live in Central Florida in Winter Haven, the water ski capital of the world.

You can reach out to Deb on her email: dschmitt12117@gmail.com or her website: www.debcrutcher.com

www.ingramcontent.com/pod-product-compliance
Lightning Source LLC
Chambersburg PA
CBHW061655120626
46550CB00003B/952